# GOD of
# MIRACLES

# Also by Jeff Barnhardt

## Destined to Be:
*Nine Keys to Live a Life of Purpose*
*While Unlocking Your Full Potential*
www.amazon.com/Destined-Be
-Purpose-Unlocking-Potential-ebook/dp/B01MU6340G

## Destined to Be Study Guide
www.amazon.com/Destined-Study-Guide
-Jeff-Barnhardt/dp/1546357572

## Destined to Be Facilitator's Guide
www.amazon.com/Destined-Facilitators-Guide
-Jeff-Barnhardt/dp/1546357629

## God of Miracles:
*Ordinary People, Extraordinary Stories*
www.amazon.com/God-Miracles
-Ordinary-Extraordinary-Stories-ebook/dp/B0786WG4QQ

# GOD of MIRACLES

## ORDINARY PEOPLE
## EXTRAORDINARY STORIES

# JEFF BARNHARDT

*God of Miracles*
© Jeff Barnhardt 2017

ISBN: 978-0-9958364-2-6 (print)
ISBN: 978-0-9958364-3-3 (ebook)

*Editor: Jocelyn Drozda*
*Cover design: Jeff Gifford*
*Interior design: Beth Shagene*

I dedicate this book to a precious two-and-a-half-year-old girl, Kailey Grace Dyck, who we lost much too early in life. Kailey was intelligent, caring, and an overall joy to have around. We love you, Kailey, and we look forward to seeing you again in Heaven.

I would also like to dedicate this book to her parents, Trisha and Brendan Dyck, who I have seen walk through the fire of loss only to become stronger. The courage and strength they have demonstrated as they face this unimaginable challenge has been an inspiration to me and to my family. Watching them continue to pursue God through all the pain has been humbling. Their willingness to talk about their loss and encourage others with their testimony is a blessing to the Kingdom of God. It has been my privilege to witness how many lives this family has impacted through this tragedy. My prayer is God would even do more, in Jesus' name.

# Contents

*Acknowledgments*                                                9

*Foreword*                                                      11

*Introduction*                                                  15

*First Things First*                                            19

CHAPTER 1:  Our Inheritance                                     21

CHAPTER 2:  Humble Beginnings and Defining
            Moments                                             35

CHAPTER 3:  From Dream to Reality                               49

CHAPTER 4:  Panama City                                         63

CHAPTER 5:  "GO!"                                               75

CHAPTER 6:  The Boardroom                                       83

CHAPTER 7:  God of Miracles                                     93

# Acknowledgments

FIRST, I WOULD LIKE TO THANK JESUS CHRIST, MY PERsonal Lord and Savior. Accepting Him as Savior was the first step on this incredible journey with the Holy Spirit. I'm so thankful to have seen what I have seen and experienced what I have experienced. There's nothing like witnessing the power of God transforming lives right before your eyes.

I would also like to thank my wife, Andrea Barnhardt, whose patience and flexibility has once again allowed me to complete the arduous task of writing a book. My appreciation also goes to my daughter, Janaya, for all the times she helped her mom while I was away on ministry trips, and my sons Jaron, Micah, and Daxton for helping out during these trips in their own special ways. My prolonged absences were not easy on my family, but they served alongside me with their sacrifice.

I'd like to thank my Pastor, Joel Wells, who has been a close friend and confidante along this journey of development. His belief in me and his willingness to extend the invitation to Africa were a critical parts of my journey. I would also like to thank Linda Wells, who has always been a constant encouragement to me, and whose confirmation of the Lord's Word to go to Africa became my invitation.

Last, but definitely not least, I'd like to thank Jocelyn Drozda, who was instrumental in the completion of this book with her hours of editing and feedback. Her willingness to devote her time to this project when I would insert a last-minute change or add a chapter after returning from a mission trip made writing this book much easier. With the inspiration of the Holy Spirit, she wrote the powerful prayers at the end of each chapter. I would highly recommend her as an editor, and even more so as a friend.

All the best,

JEFF BARNHARDT

# Foreword

A S A CHILD GROWING UP IN A PASTOR'S HOME, I WAS fascinated with the power of God. My father used to give me biographies to read of great men and women who had been used by God in extraordinary ways. As I read these books, I dreamed of one day God using me in the same way. However, as I grew older, I found myself becoming more cynical and my simple faith in God was challenged. I had experienced some disappointments in areas where I didn't see the power of God as I was expecting to see it. This left me somewhat confused and discouraged.

However, as the years have gone by, I have become convinced of the goodness of God and have learned to trust him even in situations where I have not understood everything. I have also been pressing into the miracle power of God and seeing God do amazing things.

In the middle of this journey I met my friend Jeff Barnhardt. When I first met him, he was in the middle of a faith crisis and in a pretty desperate place in his life. He will share some of his journey with you in this book. Early on in our relationship, God used me to help put back the pieces of his faith and his relationship with God. As Jeff's confidence in God began to grow, so did our friendship, and Jeff and I have begun to contend together for the purposes of God. Proverbs 27:17 says, *As iron sharpens iron, so a friend sharpens a friend.* Jeff and I have this kind of friendship. We are always pushing each other to be who God has called us to be and to dream big.

Truth be told, Jeff is like a burr under my saddle sometimes. He has become so convinced in the ability of God to do above and beyond what we can ask or think, that he always wants to take another radical step of faith. He is a hard guy to keep up with! Jeff has pushed me to believe in my own gifting and calling and has provoked me to contend for the supernatural.

I am now a crusade evangelist and Jeff accompanies me on many of my crusades. He is always standing to the side of the stage praying for the sick and seeing God do amazing things. I told him at our last crusade to pray and ask God to tell him the miracles he was going to do that night so I could call them out. It was my turn to provoke him to push deeper into his prophetic gifting! One of the situations God revealed to him was a man, blind in his right eye, that God wanted to heal. After preaching, I asked for such a man to identify himself and when he came forward for prayer, Jeff and I stood side-by-side and prayed for him. As we prayed together, this man's eye went from totally blind, to being able to identify the numbers on our cell phone. I'm not sure who was more excited, Jeff and I, or the man who was healed!

This book is filled with stories such as this and Jeff will share with you his own journey that led him from tragedy to faith and the release of God's power. This book will not give you all the answers and in fact, it may provoke even more questions, but I believe it will become a Holy irritant in your life. I pray it will provoke you to believe God and give you a platform to launch out in greater faith in your own life. God wants to display his miracle power through you! Get ready to be challenged and get ready to go!

JOEL WELLS
Lead Pastor
Harvest City Church
Regina, Sk. Canada

# Introduction

FOR THE FIRST FIFTEEN YEARS OF MY CHRISTIAN LIFE, I possessed a form of godliness, but I denied its power. I did not believe in miracles, for what seemed to be a valid reason. I spent years watching people receive prayer and claim God healed their back, big toe, or something else equally indiscernible to an observer. I had never witnessed a paralyzed person rising from a wheelchair or deaf ears being opened. During that time, I wasn't fully convinced they were actually healed. I am not saying they weren't healed; I just had a hard time believing they were.

Perhaps this was because I too, was standing in those same prayer lines, and nothing happened for me. I had been prayed for literally hundreds of times by dozens of people, both ordinary churchgoers, and giants of the faith. I have had quiet prayers, loud prayers, English prayers and prayers in tongues—all for the same thing—for my blind eyes to be opened. But each time, nothing had happened.

Frustration emerged as what I knew to be true in the

Bible, the infallible Word of God, was not manifesting in my own life experience. The gospels are riddled with documentation of Jesus healing all the people in a vast crowd. More specifically, he opened the eyes of multiple blind men, most notably Bartimaeus, as they raised their voices and cried out to Him for mercy. But my head knowledge conflicted with that of my heart. I know it could happen, but *Why hasn't it happened for me? Why have I not been healed?* I began to think maybe miracles were for the past, but not for today.

I remember trying to muster up enough faith to believe my eyes would be healed, thinking I was the problem. Maybe I had missed repenting for something in my past, or I needed to increase my confessions. Maybe I needed to fast more often, or raise my voice and cry out to Jesus like blind Bartimaeus had done. Nothing worked! The answer eluded me. There did not seem to be a formula I could apply to make it happen. These experiences left me feeling disappointed, hurt, disillusioned, and bitter. I thus spent the first fifteen years of my Christian life being very cynical in regard to miracles—especially those involving physical healing. My cynicism continued until God sovereignly revealed to me His miracle-working power. These incredibly tangible experiences I am about to share with you migrated the belief in miracles the needed eighteen inches from my mind to my heart. Now from the abundance of my heart, my mouth—or this book, rather—shall speak!

I am still astonished, but very thankful, that God has

chosen a visually impaired former doubter like myself, to witness so many incredible miracles. My own insecurities and sense of insignificance held me back far too long. I am the most unlikely person for God to have used—but He did! This fact is what makes this book so powerful. The wondrous news is that God is not a respecter of persons—it doesn't matter who you are—He will do miracles in and through your life as well.

In this book, the Holy Spirit and I will take you on a journey through seven incredible, real life miracles, paired with seven powerful prayers to equip you to reach for miracles in your own life. It is not about applying some magical system to see miracles happen; it is about bringing down the barriers hindering them. Perhaps you believe God does not need people to perform miracles; He is sovereign and can perform them at will. This is true, but the Bible states that Jesus did not perform many miracles in Nazareth because of their lack of faith (Matthew 13:58). There is absolutely, by God's sovereign choice, a human participation in the working of miracles. We do not perform miracles, God does, but we can definitely be a conduit for that to happen.

The facts concerning the miracles presented are true, though some names have been changed or excluded to protect the identity of those in vulnerable situations. The miraculous events range from life transformations to physical healings. I hold great reverence for miracles, and I am therefore not interested in disingenuous ones. If you are cynical like I had been and would like to see some proof of them, several of these miracles have been captured on video and can be viewed on my website at *www.jeffbarnhardt.com*.

My prayer is that this book will not only encourage you to believe for your own miracles, but will also empower you to pray for others to receive theirs. If you are like I had been, believing in your mind for miracles, but not in your heart, I pray this book will help you move from head knowledge to heart experience. My hope is that you do not have to live like I had for so long, with a form of godliness, but denying its power. At the end of each chapter, I align with you in prayer to help you overcome common barriers to unleashing miracles in your life. The book ends with a commissioning prayer to activate both the gift of faith and the working of miracles through you. My prayer is that as you read and pray, your heart will be stirred to believe and unleash the miracle-working power of God!

# First Things First

MIRACLES ARE FANTASTIC! HOWEVER, IT IS FAR MORE important to connect with the miracle worker, Jesus Christ. If you do not know Him as your personal Lord and Savior, I ask you to join with me in a simple prayer to invite Him to be the miracle worker in your life. In verbalizing the following prayer, you will experience the miracle of salvation, taking you from the darkness into the light, so you will be able to enjoy the free gift of eternal life.

PRAYER:

> *"Dear Jesus, I believe You died on the cross for my sin, and through Your death, You have extended to me forgiveness and grace. Please forgive me of my sin and come into my heart. Be the Lord of my life. In Jesus' name, I pray. Amen."*

If you prayed the above prayer for the first time or

recommitted your life to Jesus, the Bible says old things are passed away, and all things are made new (2 Corinthians 5:17 NKJV). You are born again! This is a new beginning for you. Let someone know you have made this commitment, then please go to my website at *www.jeffbarnhardt.*com and send me a message. I would love to agree with you in prayer!

# CHAPTER ONE

# Our Inheritance

GOD LOVES TO PERFORM MIRACLES THROUGH HIS people; so much so that He paid the ultimate price—sacrificing His Son—to make this possible. But before Jesus went to the cross, He exemplified for us how to walk in God's miracle-working power. He performed countless miracles, vastly diverse in nature; from those of provision—the feeding of 5000, to miracles of healing, such as blind eyes opening and the lame walking. And within this diversity of miracles, each account illustrates the new and creative ways in which He performed them.

These miracles effectively demonstrate that God will use each individual in a unique manner in all aspects of our faith life, but especially in the working of miracles. Though many of us readily believe that Jesus, as the Son of God, can, of course, work miracles, we can be hesitant to believe *regular people* can do the same. Yet Jesus explicitly said that we will do the same things as He did, and even greater (John 14:12). To fully understand how this is possible, we must start with the finished work of the cross.

Jesus' name means *to save*, which is precisely what was accomplished through His death on the cross: whoever will believe in their heart and confess with their mouth that Jesus Christ is Lord, shall be saved (Romans 10:9). In Greek, the word *saved* is "sózó." According to Strong's Online Concordance, *sózó* means to save, deliver, protect, heal, preserve, do well, and to be made whole (4982). When Jesus died on the cross to save us, He paid the price for our passage to Heaven, *and* to make us whole. This enables us to live a prosperous life, full of power, while still living on earth.

To live this life of power, we must first understand that it is only by *faith*, through *grace*, that we can receive the gift of salvation. "Faith is the substance of things hoped for, the evidence of things not seen" (Hebrews 11:1 NKJV), and the good news is God has given every man a measure of faith (Romans 12:3). We are then able to apply this measure of faith, through *grace*, to receive our free gift of salvation. *Grace* is firstly, the *unmerited favor of God*. Romans 3:23 tells us all fall short of the glory of God, and it is only through His *grace*, His unmerited favor, He has chosen us. But *grace* is also the power of God that works through us to help us accomplish the things He has called us to do on this earth. In Hebrews 10:29, the differing translations of the Bible interchange the term the *Spirit of Grace*, and the *Holy Spirit*. The Holy Spirit—the Spirit of Grace—is part of the gift we receive upon salvation. When we receive Christ, the Holy Spirit joins with our own spirit, helping to bring us to salvation.

Before Jesus ascended to Heaven, He told His disciples that He had to go so One greater than Him could come

(John 16:7). The One to whom Jesus refers is the Holy Spirit—the power of God on earth today. Immediately after giving the disciples the Great Commission in Matthew 28, Jesus implored the disciples not to leave Jerusalem until they receive this promised gift of the Holy Spirit. The fact that they would not be released until then indicates that we also require the Holy Spirit and His power to fulfill that same commission. Jesus' words that John baptized in water, but they would be baptized in the Holy Spirit, attests to a difference between the infilling of the Holy Spirit upon salvation, and the baptism of the Holy Spirit.

The most informative explanation I've heard for this concept is like this: when you drink a glass of water, that water is now *inside* of you. If you go to the ocean and jump in, you would then be *inside* the water. Upon salvation, you are given a drink of the Holy Spirit. With the baptism of the Holy Spirit, the drink pours out from you, completely surrounding you with the water. The initial drink of the Holy Spirit produces the life of Jesus in you. The baptism of the Holy Spirit pouring out from you reproduces the ministry of Jesus through you. Therefore, even though you may have received salvation, the baptism of the Holy Spirit is imperative. The good news is that this is a promised gift from the Lord, available to all believers!

Ephesians 1:14 tells us the Holy Spirit is a deposit of the inheritance the Father has for us. Therefore, as believers in Christ, co-heirs of this inheritance, we have a right to the Holy Spirit's incredible power that is manifested in the nine spiritual gifts. These gifts are just that—they are gifts. The

Bible says God gives them to us freely and without repentance (1 Corinthians 2:12, Romans 11:29). They are provided to the body of Christ for the purpose of expanding the Kingdom of God on earth.

One of these spiritual gifts is the working of miracles. Therefore, if the Holy Spirit is on earth with these nine incredible spiritual gifts available to the whole body, why are *all* believers not walking in this miracle-working power? It's simply because we, as part of the body of Christ, do not understand our identity and authority in Jesus.

We possess a form of godliness but deny it's power. We do not allow the power of the Holy Spirit to flow through us. We pray, begging God to heal us or those around us. We cry out with loud and long prayers, attempting to convince God to provide for our needs. Yet, we miss the truth that the Father has already provided a great inheritance for us; an inheritance so great it not only supplies enough to meet our every physical, emotional, mental, and spiritual need, but immense enough to meet the needs of the entire world. Our Father has unlimited resources made available to you through Jesus and the Holy Spirit. Every follower of Christ has been given a key from the Father to access this amazing inheritance.

Too many believers today have a finite mindset, thinking there's only so much of God's power and resources to go around. They perhaps believe He only uses *special* people for the working of miracles and for the expansion of His Kingdom. However, the Bible clearly states that we should all desire spiritual gifts (1 Corinthians 14:1). God is not a respecter of people—He shows no partiality (Acts 10:34). If you are a believer, He wants to provide you with all the needed resources, and He earnestly desires that His miracle-working power flows through you! The truth is He is a God of great abundance and He has more than enough for everyone. God is a good Father and He gives us good things. And if the Holy Spirit and His power is only a deposit of our inheritance ... wow! How much more is there to come?

Let us think about this Holy Spirit inheritance for a moment in concrete terms. Going through life as a believer without receiving the fullness of your salvation, which includes the power of the Holy Spirit, is like being given a car by your loving Father, complete with an unlimited supply of gas, and the access key, yet never even attempting to engage the engine! Your salvation in Christ represents the vehicle. The Holy Spirit represents the gas, which powers it forward. But you need to use the key to access it, which is *faith*. If you never use the key to start the car, you'll never experience the incredible joy of the gift, nor its intended function. Though the car is an amazing blessing in itself, without the key and the gas, you are not going anywhere, thus failing to fully impact not only your life, but the lives of those around you.

On the other side of the equation, the devil does not want us to know our identity in Christ, nor the power of the inheritance we have been given through the Holy Spirit. He is more than happy to keep us asking God for things He has already given to us. Truthfully, if we are busy continually asking, we are prevented from acting upon it. However, we should understand that it is completely appropriate to ask God to move on our behalf in our individual circumstances and situations. Asking for wisdom, guidance, and for God to fight for us is scriptural. After all, we are in a spiritual war. But we must learn to pray from the right position; the position of authority.

Ephesians 2:6 tells us we are seated in heavenly places with Christ Jesus. This heavenly seat is one of authority and dominion; one that is over all things, both in Heaven and on earth. We must pray in the name of Jesus, exercising faith, believing He is a rewarder of those who diligently seek Him (Hebrews 11:6). We must pray, believing we will receive that for which we are contending. First Peter 2:24 tells us, in fact, that we are already healed by the stripes of Jesus. It is always His will that all are healed, a matter that was settled by the cross. It isn't suggested we *might be*, or we're *going to be*, but that we are *already* healed. Do not forget that when Jesus died, He brought salvation—meaning *wholeness*—to us, which includes complete spiritual, emotional, mental, and physical health.

Early in my Christian walk, this posed a great personal dilemma. If I was supposedly already healed, how come I still could not see? If people are supposed to be already healed, why do we even need to pray for them? The reality is, when Adam and Eve chose to partake of the fruit from the tree of knowledge of good and evil in the garden, they gave the devil dominion and authority over the earth. The result was that the earth, now in its fallen state, began to experience deterioration, including sickness, disease, and death.

Through His mercy and grace, the Father had already planned a way to rectify this fallen state. Ephesians 1 explains that it was His plan from the beginning of time to bring us into His family through Jesus Christ. When Jesus died on the cross, He went to hell and defeated the devil, taking back all authority. He then rose to Heaven and sent the Holy Spirit to be His power on the earth. When we accept Jesus as Lord of our life, we acquire this authority and possess the dominion over the earth, through Christ.

It is thus the job of the believer to exercise this authority and enforce the dominion of Christ throughout the earth. To thoroughly understand how this can be accomplished, let's explore it through another avenue. Imagine that the gift of the car to which was previously referred, is actually a police car. The Father is the King of all the land, and we are simply enforcing His authority that He has vested in us. Through our identity now as His police officers, we have been given power, authority, and weapons to take down the enemy. In the same manner, exercising our faith and praying in the name of Jesus evokes the Holy Spirit's power to bring the Kingdom down to earth; the principles and laws of Heaven, such as healing, will thus manifest on earth. We must declare the authority of Christ over every situation, and bring all of His enemies into captivity.

Second Corinthians 10:4 tells us the weapons of our warfare are not carnal, but mighty to bring down strongholds, powers and principalities. That is why, in the name of Jesus Christ, we have the power to command demons to flee. And that is why we can lay hands on the sick and they shall recover. We must step out in this authority that comes from our identity in Christ. On our own we cannot heal anyone; but in Christ, with the power and authority that comes through Him and the Holy Spirit, we are able to work miracles. Therefore, as a believer, you can have great confidence that when you pray for the sick, they are indeed, healed!

However, it does not suffice to say there will never be spiritual battles when we pray for healing. The spiritual battle may even cause a physical manifestation in the person's body. For example, when I pray for someone's pain and the pain moves, there is usually a demon involved. When this happens, we need to use our authority in Christ to cast the demon out and command the dominion of Christ to take hold in the person's body. We have the right, as believers, to bind up demons and cast them out. Sickness and disease are criminals trespassing in places they do not belong; they have no jurisdiction. It is our job, much like a spiritual police officer, to arrest them and command them to leave.

Moreover, the authority and dominion of Christ is not only for casting out demons. We also have authority to speak to the body and command it to be healed, in Jesus' name, and it must obey. I used to think that this was a very rude and insensitive manner in which to pray for someone. This way of thinking remained until I had a very powerful experience while praying for the sick in Uganda.

I was part of a ministry team hosting a community

crusade in a rural town of about 30,000 people. The spiritual warfare was intense. Part of the attack was a huge afternoon rainstorm that muddied the field and caused large puddles to cover an area of about sixty feet in front of the stage. The rain drenched many of the main speakers, forcing us to remedy the situation with hair dryers. This delayed the worship team—they could not be used to usher in the presence of the Holy Spirit before my pastor, Joel Wells, preached. Regardless, he powered through and delivered a great message to a crowd which, due to the unrelenting rain of the afternoon, was somewhat smaller than the previous night.

After the message, despite the efforts of the enemy, approximately one hundred people gave their lives to Christ, and hundreds of others descended upon the altar for healing prayer. As I prayed for people through an interpreter, it felt extremely difficult to break through the enemy's strongholds. But regardless of our feelings, God is faithful. Several people received healing. Thinking I was finished praying for the evening, my interpreter intercepted my exit, requesting that I pray for a lady who had been carried to the event by her family.

No sooner was the word "Yes" out of my mouth when intimidation sought to sabotage me. But as I walked to where she was on the ground, with her family at her side, I heard the Holy Spirit ensure me He would heal her. Though it was dark and hard for me to see, I placed my hands on her and began to pray. I heard the Holy Spirit tell me to say, "Stand, in Jesus' name!" Reluctance gripped my heart at this request, because of my own past experiences as others prayed for me. With the persistence of the Holy Spirit, I was obedient, and said, "Stand, in Jesus' name!" And ... she stood up! To be completely honest, it surprised me. I had to take a few steps back to regain my composure and to pray.

Then my interpreter exclaimed, "She is stepping! She is stepping!" The crowd erupted into spontaneous cheering! Holding both of her hands, I began to walk backwards, with her following me! I kept saying, "Jesus ... Walk in the name of Jesus!" My interpreter kept repeating, "She is stepping, she is stepping!" followed by, "She is walking! She is walking! She is smiling! She is smiling!" At that moment, the lady let go of my hands and the interpreter proclaimed, "She is clapping! She is clapping!"

I placed my hand on her forehead and began to pray again. Though words do not suffice, the only way I can explain what I felt was that it was like surges of electricity were going through my body, and she began to vibrate. As the interpreter suddenly blurted, "She is dancing! She is dancing!" the crowd burst into wild excitement, praising God! I began to dance too, shouting and giving glory to God! Upon speaking to the family, it was confirmed that she had been bedridden for over a year and had not been able to walk at all. After navigating the steps of the stage, she then gave her testimony! All glory to God. He is the healer!

This experience is one example of using the authority given to me through my identity in Christ. Since Jesus had already paid the price for her healing, as a believer, my job was to obediently pray and declare the Kingdom of God to come to her life.

The question remains, however, what if you pray for someone, take authority, cast out the demons, and there is no apparent healing? Jesus has paid the price for all of us to be healed. When we pray and believe for that healing, we are healed. Period. The major difference is the timing in which the healing manifests. Some people are healed instantly. I have also seen evidence of healing emerge in one, two, and even three days. Some people's healing does not manifest until they go to Heaven. Regardless of when it materializes, they are healed. It is only the issue of timing that is in question. For this reason, it is imperative to pray, no matter what you feel or see, don't feel or don't see. Remember, you are praying in the authority given to you from your identity in Christ. Your prayer is bringing the dominion of God to the earth—bringing Heaven to earth. And that is miraculous!

## INSIGHT:

It is possible to have accepted Christ, but to have not yet received the baptism of the Holy Spirit. Although we may be going to Heaven, we are denying the power on earth that can change our life, and that of many others around us. Through the combination of the power of the Holy Spirit, and the authority and dominion given to us through our identity in Christ, there is no weapon formed against us that can prosper! Not even the gates of hell can withstand us!

If you have not received the baptism of the Holy Spirit, I recommend you request it of the Lord by praying the following prayer. This can be followed up by asking a pastor, church leader, or a friend who has received this gift to lay hands on you and pray for you to receive the baptism of the Holy Spirit. Remember, this is a free gift from a good Father; all you need to do is receive it. Take courage and be bold! You have the authority and power that raised Christ from the grave in you!

## Prayer:

*Thank you for the gifts of salvation, faith and grace. Thank you, especially, for the gift of Your Son, Jesus. Thank you that I am able to access this amazing inheritance of the Holy Spirit.*

*Father, please forgive me for being complacent and not seeking after all You have available to me; the fullness of my salvation. I ask for Your wisdom and guidance in all things. Increase my faith in believing You hear my prayers, and You respond, bringing spiritual, emotional, mental, and physical healing and wholeness.*

*Help me to understand and to exercise my identity and my position of authority in Christ. Help me to enforce the dominion of Christ throughout the earth, taking down the enemy and setting captives free— expanding Your Kingdom on the earth. Teach me to boldly step out in the authority that brings down strongholds, powers, and principalities, and causes demons to flee!*

*I desire the power of the Holy Spirit to flow through me; I desire Your miracle-working power. Lord, I ask You to baptize me in the power of the Holy Spirit. Lord, Thy Kingdom come! I pray this in Jesus' name. Amen.*

# CHAPTER TWO

# Humble Beginnings and Defining Moments

WATCHING THE HIGHLIGHT REEL OF THE MIRACLES experienced by others can be intriguing. What we see can inspire us or discourage us—or both. We can be encouraged to step out, only to become discouraged as the results are not what we had anticipated. We must understand, however, that the majority of believers who now walk in miracle-working power and authority originally started out from a place of humble beginnings.

This is true with myself. As previously stated, to every man is given a measure of faith. It is up to us to exercise our faith, along with our authority and dominion, to see the Kingdom of God come to earth. Like a muscle, as faith is exercised it will grow and become stronger. This process is not easy and it will definitely develop your character. The good news is the faith you develop in this process, along with the character, will help you fulfill your calling. The remainder of this book walks through several different types of miracles in which I have personally been an active participant. To do my part in these miracles I had to apply and stretch my faith, and step-by-step it grew. In this next chapter, we will step back several years to a very difficult time in the lives of my family and I—my place of humble beginnings.

There are times in our lives when we are defined by events in ways we cannot comprehend while in their midst. These situations challenge the very core of who we are as believers, and even as human beings. Often, we only recognize their sheer impact when we peer at our life through the lens of hindsight. Only then do we see the powerful hand of God at work, masterfully weaving the hardest of life's circumstances into a beautiful tapestry. We then can see through the lens of reflection how deep His love is, and how He causes all things to work together for our good. My family was directly confronted by one such event that would leave us forever changed.

It was during the month of May. My wife Andrea and I, had just started our first business together. The air was electric. We had recently purchased a new home, and everything was progressing favorably. Then we received the type of phone call every person dreads. Andrea's sister called to tell us our young niece, Kailey Grace, was in the hospital. Andrea immediately decided to go to their city to support her sister. I was extremely busy with the newly formed company, making it very difficult to leave. This forced my wife to travel the two hours alone. Shortly after Andrea had arrived, the doctors moved Kailey to the ICU and put her on life-support. We quickly realized the situation was critical, and because of this change in circumstance, I too, made the trek.

Arriving at the hospital, I proceeded to the ICU family

waiting room. It was filled with family members, some who had been holding vigil for days. I immediately wanted to see Kailey so I could lay hands on her and pray—hoping and believing God would miraculously heal her. I was caught off guard when we had to scrub and put on special suits to even go in the room. Once scrubbed up and robes donned, we entered the room and that's where I saw beautiful Kailey Grace, laying on the bed. She had contracted meningitis and had now been in the hospital for several days. She was intubated, and her eyes were closed. She honestly looked like a little angel. I remember her beautiful hair with the cutest little curls.

With tears in my eyes, I laid my hands on her and began to pray, asking God to do a miracle … asking God to heal this little girl. Many people were still praying and weeping in the waiting room when I returned. One family member approached me, put their arm around my shoulders, and said, "We're going to have to let go." I was horrified, because I truly believed God would heal her. Why wouldn't He? She was an innocent, beautiful, little girl. At this point the wrestling in my heart began. *Did I really believe He would heal her?*

Not long afterward, some of the hospital staff called everyone into the room. The doctor and the social worker informed us about Kailey's condition. They explained how the cognitive scale works: normal brain activity was ten, while no brain activity was registered as zero. They informed us Kailey's brain activity was zero on the scale. People burst into sobs around the room; I couldn't believe it. I had been praying for her for days before coming, and as I had laid hands on her, I had prayed my best faith prayer.

Kailey was only two-and-a-half years old. This amazing child was definitely one of the smartest little girls I had ever met in my life. She did the funniest old-man-impressions you would ever have heard. She was quick-witted and super-cute. I had always felt like there was something inherently special about Kailey. My heart in turmoil, I thought, *This could not be happening.* I could not accept this devastating news. I could not accept that a loving, caring God would take such a precious little girl from us. Unfortunately, she was indeed taken from us by this terrible illness.

The heart-wrenching decision was made to unplug her from the life-support system. I remember being in the room with the family as they walked through this trau-matic, life-altering event. I do not think it was planned, but I remember the lyrics of the song playing on the DVD player at the time were, *He gives and takes away . . . Blessed be the name of the Lord.* I am still unsure if it was actually playing, or if it was just playing on the soundtrack in my mind, but to this day that song transports me back to that time, to that room. The tears flowed abundantly, and that moment was quite possibly the most excruciating pain I've ever felt in my life. I had never cried so hard, for so long, as I did that day. Looking around the room, the sheer agony of my loved ones was apparent—too much to bear. But bear it, we did.

My seemingly unanswered prayer rocked my faith to the core and sent me into a very dark and challenging place for several years. I had already been struggling with the reality of healing miracles, but now I was confronted head-on with the questions of "Is God good?" and, "Does He love me at all?"

The years that followed were full of many trials, pain, and tears. The truth was, I was angry at God and felt I could not trust Him. It was hard for me to comprehend why such a terrible thing could happen so unjustly. The circumstances seemed cruel, and I found it unbelievably difficult to move forward. I disconnected myself, to a great extent, from the things of God, and I instead threw myself into my work. The lack of connection to God led to an extremely tumultuous time for my marriage and my family.

Regardless, the hands of time relentlessly marched on, and my son, Micah, was born. We love our little guy beyond words, and at six-months-old, he became sick. After he had been running a fever for a few days, we took him to the doctor and she quickly referred him to a pediatrician for an examination. While booking the appointment with the pediatrician's office, I informed the receptionist that his fontanel—the soft spot located at the top of his head—was so swollen it was forming a small triangular point, and his nose was running. Since Kailey's passing, our entire family refuses to take risks when it comes to young children's health. The receptionist, with some urgency in her voice, asked if we were in the city and if we could come in immediately. I'm not sure if it was the words she voiced or the urgency of the tone, but I could not help feeling nervous.

I disconnected and we instantly packed up our young son and were off to the doctor's office.

As we hurried through the streets, the all-too-familiar sinking feeling in the pit of my stomach returned. We were quickly ushered into an examination room upon arrival. As it turned out, the pediatrician who would be seeing Micah had also had Kailey in his care while she was hospitalized with meningitis. He entered the room and immediately began examining our son. After about sixty seconds, he looked at us and gravely said, "You need to go to the hospital as quickly as possible. Do not stop anywhere, just go straight there. I think your son has meningitis." He told us he would phone the emergency room in advance so they would be prepared for our arrival.

In that moment time stopped, then everything went into slow-motion. Fear gripped our hearts. We had seen this movie before and we knew the ending. I couldn't believe it; I think my body went into shock. My wife and I burst into inconsolable tears. We knew precisely what that horrible word meant. We gathered up our son and headed to our vehicle. On the way to the hospital, everything continued in slow motion. *How could this be happening? This was unreal!* We made the incredibly difficult phone call to the family; I could barely get the words out of my mouth through the tears. They rushed to meet us at the hospital.

Upon arriving at the emergency room, we ran up to the desk, urgently requesting that Micah be admitted without delay. However, the clerk insisted we had to fill out the paperwork first. While my frustration began to bubble up and overflow, a nurse swooped in from behind the desk and asked if this was Micah. I confirmed it was and immediately she scooped him up and ran down the hall. Finishing the paperwork, we rushed into the room he was in—room number one. The emergency wing has a room-number sequence from one to thirty-five. Patients are allocated based on the seriousness of their illness; being placed in room number one was a grave indication of Micah's condition.

By the time we completed the paperwork and entered Micah's room, Andrea's parents, Dale and Patti, were already present. There we were once again, in a hospital room, with a baby hooked up to tubes. The shock of it was overwhelming and the tears, of course, flowed freely. *I can't believe it. How can we be in this situation again?*

One of the hardest things I have ever had to watch in my life was the nurses putting my little baby down for the required spinal tap to test for meningitis. His screams of pain were hard to endure. That agony was followed by a CT scan. Two very powerful antibiotics were introduced into his body to fight back against the possible meningitis. Before too long, they had admitted him into the pediatric ward. They brought us upstairs to an isolation room where as a precaution, we once again had to don special robes and scrub before entering the room. It was hard to fathom, but this was the exact hospital in which Kailey had passed away. As I write these words now, I am struggling to find the right ones to possibly express the depth of feelings and torrent of emotions in which we were drowning while enduring such an unbelievable situation for the second time. *How could this be happening to our family? How could this utter nightmare be occurring all over—again?*

The doctor entered the room holding a file folder in his hand. The results of the spinal tap had come back negative for meningitis. Relief washed over us, but the doctor was not finished. The folder also contained the CT scan of Micah's brain. He pointed out an area where there was fluid on the brain and where one of the ventricles was swollen. He said they thought it was bleeding, and pressure was building. They had already paged the pediatric neurosurgeon. They were going to have to perform emergency brain surgery on him that night to alleviate the swelling.

At that moment, I was slammed face-first into a faith crisis. I found myself crying out to God to have mercy on my son. Last time, my prayers didn't get the response I expected, so I reached out to my friends. I phoned my pastor, Joel Wells, and he brought with him another Pastor, Dwayne Allan. Joel and Dwayne quickly arrived. These two men were close personal friends of mine, so I knew I could let my guard down. A fresh surge of tears therefore resurfaced upon sight of them. They scrubbed up, put on the special suits, and went in to pray for Micah. They laid hands on him and asked God to do a miracle.

About an hour and a half later, the pediatric neurosurgeon arrived. He walked into the room holding the same file folder as the previous doctor. He asked us why he was required. This was a huge shock; certainly not what I expected to hear. I explained, as if I was an authority

on the matter, there was bleeding on Micah's brain causing swelling and that immediate surgery was essential. He
responded with, "No, we do not need to do surgery. He is
okay. There is nothing wrong with Micah."

I was stunned! *What had just happened? Maybe they
missed something.* A flood of very cautious optimism crept
over me at that moment in time. *Had God healed him? Or
maybe there was something else wrong.* We waited for the
pediatrician to come back. He returned and assessed the
situation, performing a complete examination of my son
once again. He could not find anything wrong. No meningitis. Confused, they proceeded to do a multitude of other
tests and … nothing! God had worked a miracle! I was
ecstatic! We were going to be able to take Micah home with
us in a couple of days! The joy lasted momentarily, as my
heart soon turned back to Kailey. Micah did not have meningitis and we still did not know what caused the fluid in
the swollen ventricle, but he was coming home. The questions came back. *Why, God, did you not do a miracle with
Kailey?*

## Insight:

Reflecting on the situation, it is clear that the enemy comes
with the intent to kill, steal, and destroy (John 10:10).
Micah did not have meningitis, but the devil used the pain
from our past experience with that illness to grip us with
fear and steal any hope we may have had going into his
hospitalization. As previously confessed, I do not know

how miracles work, but I do know that God does them. When I arrive in Heaven, will I have questions for Jesus? Absolutely. But I have learned that God is good! Even if we do not understand it at the time, He will use every situation to work together for good. I explore this concept more thoroughly in my book *Destined to Be: Nine Keys to Live a Life of Purpose While Unlocking Your Full Potential.*

God did not take Kailey. He received her into His presence, and that is a big difference. If God has not answered your prayer in the way you were hoping for and you have not received your miracle, please understand that God does not make bad things happen to good people; the devil does. But God, through His mercy and grace, will deliver us from them all. Though I prayed for Kailey's miracle in faith, I did not get the answer I wanted. But this does not change the fact that God is good and He is a God of miracles. Salvation, the gracious gift of eternal life is the most incredible miracle of all. Although it was hard to understand this when Kailey was sick and even harder to receive while enduring the incredible pain of her death, I have now come to understand Kailey is with Jesus and is completely healed. I look forward to the day when we will meet again.

Looking back at these past events through the lens of hindsight, I realized that the devil had used the situation to take me out of the game. He effectively stopped me (temporarily) from going after what I felt God had called me to do. Salvation is *opting in*. You choose to accept Jesus' forgiveness and make Him the Lord of your life. In return, you follow through on your commitment to give your life to Him and you obey the calling He gives you. By becoming so bitterly disappointed at Kailey's death, I chose to *opt out*, to not participate in, nor go after the things God had called me to do. That kept me in the wilderness for a very long time. After Micah was healed, I finally realized God is good all the time, and He is worth pursuing. That is when I chose to *opt in* to all the things He has for me and all He has called me to do. The enemy will try to use our disappointment to stop us from engaging with the significant life God has for us. We need to take authority over the enemy, then wait to see what God will do. It is then we are positioned to receive our breakthrough.

## PRAYER:

*Heavenly Father, thank you that You are at work bringing about the masterplan for my life. I surrender myself to this plan. I want to be defined solely by how You see me, and who You created me to be. Thank you for causing all things to work together for my good, and for the good of those around me. You are a good God, and You love your children so much. Lord God, increase my faith to believe this with my whole heart, even when I don't understand the things that happen. Your thoughts are higher than my thoughts, and Your ways higher than my ways, so I can only trust You in all those raw moments.*

*Lord, I repent for all the times I became angry with You when my prayers seemed unheard, unanswered, or answered in a way that was not what I wanted or expected it to be. Father, forgive me. I cast out all doubt that crept into my heart during those times. I bind up any fears. Replace all doubt and fear with faith, peace, hope, and trust in You. In any situation of disappointment where I have allowed a root of bitterness to grow, I ask You to remove it, Lord, and forgive me for thinking I know better than You. I will not allow any bitter root to tether me to the ground, nor keep me from moving forward. I repent for any place where I have walked in disobedience in anything You have called me to do.*

*Dear Lord, keep me fully engaged with You in every aspect of my life. I desire to partner with You to walk fully in the plans You have laid out for me. I believe in miracles, and I ask that You teach me to be a conduit to bring the miracles of Heaven down to earth. Open my eyes so that I might see, and my ears so that I might hear Your heart for Your people. You are Lord of my life, so I give it to You. I commit to obeying the call You have on my life. Holy Spirit, come and wash me anew. Allow Your miracle-working power to flow in and through my life. I will pursue You with all my heart and with all my soul. In Jesus' name, Amen.*

# CHAPTER THREE

# From Dream to Reality

SOMETIMES MIRACLES HAPPEN IN THE MOST UNLIKELY of places and begin in the most unexpected ways. One of these unforeseen beginnings came to pass through a dream. This was not the typical bad dream you can get from eating too much pizza before bed; I'm referring to a *prophetic dream*. A prophetic dream is one where God speaks to you, usually about future events. These dreams can be literal, but sometimes they require interpretation. We see this type of dream appear several times throughout the Bible. The most famous example is in Genesis 41, when Pharaoh dreamt about the cows and the wheat sheaves. Joseph was brought to him from prison to interpret this dream. Joseph's interpretation warned Pharaoh that there were seven years of abundance to come, followed by seven years of famine. Even though God showed Pharaoh the future through this prophetic dream, it was still Pharaoh's decision whether or not to take action.

I have experienced such prophetic dreams from time to time in my life. I find these dreams tend to be much more vivid and life-like than a regular dream. I also remember them more distinctly. One such night, I dreamt I was in an

African village. A friend of mine was giving me a tour of the area, and there was garbage strewn all around. I began to help the people pick up the garbage piece by piece, but the more I picked up, the bigger the piles became. It soon became overwhelming. Then in the dream, I saw myself standing before a crowd of African people, declaring the gospel. As I was preaching to the crowd, the power of God fell. The entire crowd was knocked over by the presence of the Holy Spirit. I then saw an image of the continent of Africa, and it was washed in blood from north to south and east to west. Then I woke up—it was three in the morning.

The dream was so real and so vivid that I recorded it on my phone. The next morning, I shared the dream with my wife and told her I thought I had to go to Africa. She looked at me and said, "Well, you're going alone." I did not tell anyone about this dream, but it stayed lodged in my heart.

One Sunday, about a year and a half later, the Lord undeniably confirmed the dream was from Him. As I was leaving the platform after helping lead worship, the wife of one of the pastors walked by me and said, "You're going to Africa." I cannot explain it, but I just burst into tears. The Holy Spirit filled my heart and confirmed my dream. It is important to understand that God will always confirm His words. He may do so through the Bible or through another individual, but He will always confirm them.

A couple of weeks later, while out for lunch with my pastor, Joel Wells, he invited me to come to Africa with him. I was stunned! I couldn't believe it. I told him I'd love to go; I just had to confirm with my wife ... but I'd love to go. My wife graciously agreed, affording me the opportunity to go to the country of Uganda with Joel the following September.

From time to time over the next few months, I went for lunch with Joel, who happens to be one of my best friends. During one of those times, he told me about Reinhard Bonnke. Reinhard is an evangelist who has preached the gospel in Africa, and has seen millions of its people come into salvation. I had never even heard of him before. Joel then told me about a school of evangelism, which Reinhard was hosting. Joel had already been accepted, and he suggested I apply. It was literally only a week before they would stop receiving applicants, but I felt I should apply. In obedience, my wife and I filled out the application and submitted it.

It was a couple of weeks later when I received the email acknowledging my acceptance! To be quite honest, I was shocked. At this point, Joel shared with me about Reinhard Bonnke's vision. He began to recount that Reinhard had had a dream about the continent of Africa being washed in blood from the north to the south, and from the east to the west—exactly how it had been in my dream! To me, this was another milestone, confirming I was definitely headed in the right direction.

We went to the conference, and it exceeded my expectations. One of the key moments was initiated when a class picture was being taken in the parking lot. Earlier in the week, Todd White had spoken on the love of God; it took all of my strength to stay in my seat and not run up to talk to him. Normally, I am not a people-chaser. I believe God can work through anyone, because He works through a guy like me. Yet there was something in my spirit urging me that having Todd pray for me was of the utmost importance. Therefore, as he began to walk back into the facility after the picture was taken, I said to him, "Todd, I'm blind. Can you pray for me?"

Without any hesitation, he grabbed me, pulled me into a hug and began to pray. His prayer evoked a cascade of fresh emotions that poured out of me. The extreme love I felt from this man made it feel as if Jesus Himself had held me. I was reduced to a mushy puddle on the parking lot pavement. I knew something had happened; something had been imparted to me.

After a while, I was able to get up from the asphalt and I made my way back into the facility. Seeing the state I was in, Joel suggested that perhaps God was not quite finished, and I should spend some time alone with Him. I agreed. Returning to the TV studio in the facility, I knelt down and prayed. The Holy Spirit came again in power and I was sobbing as He began to minister to my spirit.

He whispered, "Jeff, you have gotten your identity from being a businessman. Now I'm going to bring you into the family business." The Lord spoke to me about how I would be seeing many signs, wonders, and miracles. It was all so difficult to comprehend because I still had not received my own sight. Despite this, it gave me the inspiration and the faith I needed to persevere and see others receive their miracles from the Lord. After the conclusion of the Reinhard

Bonnke School of Evangelism, Joel and I returned home to prepare for the upcoming crusades in Africa.

September came, and our ministry team travelled to the city of Kampala, in the country of Uganda. The district was called Luzira. The crusade was going to take place on a flat, red dirt plain that had been packed down from hundreds of years of foot traffic. The red African dirt sticks to everything, especially your shoes. The stage platform was covered by a large metal roof, supported by four metal poles. To the east there were various shops with vendors selling their wares. To the left of the platform was a hill that went up about thirty feet. On the top of this hill were businesses—notorious ones. There was a gentleman's club, a gambling house, and a bar. To the right and behind the platform was a flat piece of land buried in garbage. Nestled in amongst the garbage were small one and two-room shacks—the slums of Kampala.

Some homes were held up by solid wooden walls, but others were just slat walls with dilapidated roofs. The air had a putrid smell from all the garbage on the ground, reminiscent of a long-neglected trash can finally being opened. The burning garbage only slightly masked the strong odor. It was not uncommon to see kids playing in the trash heap, despite the unappealing atmosphere. It pulled on my heart.

When I first walked onto the field by the platform, a dozen or so small African children swarmed me within seconds, touching and petting the hair on my arms. I love the African people. They are so warm and inviting to outsiders. I tried to make the little ones feel welcome and even played games with them. Some of the children would simply come up to me and hold my hand as I walked around. In some ways, it brought me back to my own childhood. I too, grew up in a very poor home, void of all luxuries and even some necessities. For me, seeing this kind of poverty was overwhelming, especially since I knew in my heart that even if I gave all I had, I couldn't change anything. That evening, as the first meeting proceeded, many people gave their lives to Jesus, but I could not shake the image of the children in the garbage.

After the meeting, we left the field and drove a short distance, where we pulled into a compound with a Western-style mall that even had a Kentucky Fried Chicken. The contrast to where we just were, was startling. It was like we drove across the world in only three blocks. While sitting down to eat chicken, I began asking questions about the locals. I learned that two-thirds of the city lived in extreme poverty. The reality of this, in practical terms, meant they only ate one meal of squashed up corn every day or two. I began to feel a sense of hopelessness coming over me. It was the helpless feeling of not being able to do anything for these people in any practical way. While the emotional tidal wave washed over me, I sat eating crisp, hot Kentucky Fried Chicken. I put the chicken down, unable to eat any more. The feeling in my gut was overtaking me, and it was more than I could bear.

That night in my hotel room, while FaceTiming with my wife, she immediately sensed something was wrong. I was very downtrodden, not myself at all. The enemy had taken ahold of my heart and shoved me into a very dark place. I began to nitpick about the team and began musing as to why I was even there. "Why do they want a blind guy that they have to lead around from place to place?" I asked. I have my peripheral vision so I can walk during the day, but at night I am completely blind. The voice in my head was telling me I was just a liability with no value to the team. I said to her, "If they want my money, I could just write a check and go home." I even went so far as to consider catching the very next available flight back home. My wife, being such an amazing woman of God, suggested I get a good-night's sleep and revisit the decision again in the morning.

I heeded her advice, and thankfully, revelation dawned with the sun. The enemy was trying, yet again, to overcome me with darkness and hopelessness. If he could convince me to go home, he would stop me from taking the next step in my destiny. With this revelation, I dropped down on my knees in the hotel room and began to pray. I said, "God, please forgive me for my lack of faith. I'll do whatever you want me to do here. I submit myself to you. Please just use me today in any way that you can." I instantly felt the heaviness lifting from me, and hope began to flood in. I realized the power of the gospel and understood that these people did not need my money; they needed a Savior. That part would change their lives, and with that part, I could help them. It was an incredible, refreshing feeling. The Bible says, "Hope deferred makes the heart sick" (Proverbs 13:12

NLT). At that moment, I realized that hope restored brings new life.

That night after a time of prayer, we headed back to the field where the meeting was to be held. I spent the majority of the evening simply standing beside the platform interceding in prayer. Near the end, my pastor, Joel Wells, had an altar call, first for salvation, and then for healing. Many, many people came forward. As I stood beside the stage with my hand on the metal support beam of the platform, I suddenly felt a small hand, that of a young African girl, go over top of mine. I found out afterwards she was five years old. I put my hand on top of hers and then she put her hand on top of my other hand and used me to guide herself around the pole that held the metal roof structure of the platform. I don't know why, but once she was in front of me I placed her two hands in a prayer position and began to bless her. After about a minute, I began to walk among the crowd. Hindered by my eyesight, I could not venture deep, but stayed within about a fifteen-foot parameter of light availed to me by the stage lights. I prayed for a few adults, but I felt nothing. I believe this lack of feeling was because the Lord wanted me elsewhere at that moment.

Walking back to the stage, I heard the Holy Spirit whisper, "Do not suffer the children to come unto Me." When I reached the stage, the same small hand, grabbed mine and pushed it to another little girl, who was leaning against the stage watching the band play. I know now this was the little girl's seven-year-old sister. Instinctively, I knew she wanted me to pray for her. I placed my hand on her shoulder and began to pray. I heard the Holy Spirit tell me to place my hands on her ears and pray for them. I was obedient to His voice and did so. As I did, I felt the power of God moving. After praying, I started back to the stage, feeling like I was finished for the night. All of a sudden, the five-year-old girl grabbed my hand again, and pulled me down to the ground where she was now sitting. In my peripheral vision, I could see her looking up at me. She was centered in the middle of a large light, glowing almost like a little angel. She said, "My eyes don't see properly." Understandably, these words were enough to shatter me into a million pieces right on the spot. Somehow, most definitely by the strength of God, I did not shatter. Instead, something rose up from inside of me, and I placed my hand over her eyes.

In my mind, I was crying out to God saying, *I can't do this! I can't believe this is happening!* But out of my mouth came drastically different words. I heard myself saying, "Sweetheart, in the Bible it says that Jesus has healed many blind people, and I believe that He can heal you too." I could feel her eyelids fluttering under my hand. I took my hand off her eyes and asked her if she could see. She looked around, and then she lit up like a million-watt light bulb. She shouted, "I can see properly!" I instantly burst into tears and began uncontrollably sobbing. She then grabbed my hand and began to point to the water bottle on the stage. I thought she wanted a drink. I called over a local lady, and she spoke to her in their native language. The little girl told the lady that before when she looked at things, it had been like looking through water. When I prayed for her, she saw two things fall off of her eyes and she now could see properly! While this was happening, the seven-year-old girl came over with another lady. She said she'd had a problem with her ears and could not hear well. When I had been praying for her, she felt a knock and then a pop in her ears, and now, she can hear properly. The miracles were documented and the girls' mother came the next night and verified them. Glory to God!

It was amazing to me how straightforward these healings were. It did not take hours of prayer or anything of the like. It was simply the power of the Holy Spirit working through a yielded, obedient person who was determined to walk into his destiny. The Bible says that God is strong in our weakness (2 Corinthians 12:10), and of this I am living proof. He used my weakness to show His strength.

## INSIGHT:

I had decided to get back into the game, but doubt was still hounding me. I'd ask myself, "What if I can't do this?" refusing to believe I could do the very thing God was calling me to do. I was, instead, believing the enemy's lie, "I can't do this." Doubt is something that can easily hold us back from experiencing the miracle-working power of God. But when we do what God calls us to do, there is grace for the calling. God will always call us to do something that is impossible to do on our own; it can only be accomplished with Jesus by our side. Doubt wants us to look at the current situation in the natural, instead of trusting and believing that Jesus wants to do the supernatural in our lives.

Many times, when miracles happen, there are multiple gifts of the body at work simultaneously. One of the key gifts I have seen coupled with miracles is a gift of *faith*. Reinhardt Bonnke often says not to pray for God to help your unbelief or doubt, rather, ask God to increase your faith. Jesus longs to do miracles in our midst and the Holy Spirit is always available to guide us and help us. We just need to have faith. Faith does not guarantee a miracle will always happen, because the miracle must align with the will and timing of God. However, our part is to have faith and God takes care of the rest, according to His timing.

I challenge you to step out, because you never know when God will perform a miracle. If you prayed for ten blind people and three were healed, would that be sufficient enough for you to step out in faith the next time you saw a blind person? What about if only two of them were healed? How about if only one of them was healed? Would you continue to take that risk and step out in faith?

## Prayer:

*Heavenly Father, thank you for desiring to partner with us in performing healing miracles. I love how You show the love of Christ to Your people, so they may be healed and set free. Let my heart be yielded to You in every way, so You can be strong in my weakness. Guide me, so I may know Your heart intimately, putting me in*

*alignment with Your will and timing in all You ask me
to do. Place in my heart a deep courage to step out in
faith. Increase this faith and grow my trust in You with
every step I take in obedience. Lord, God, please align
the events, steps, people, and resources I need that will
teach me, support me, and impart to me all that I need
to go to every place you have called me. I want to walk
in all You have for me.*

*Please reveal any areas of my life where I have
become hard, or distracted, or have wrongly derived
my identity. Help me instead, turn my focus onto
Jesus. Lord, please break off any doubt that is sent to
discourage me. I stand against any lies of the enemy that
whisper, "I'm not good enough," or "I have no value."
Forgive me for any lack of faith! I submit to Your will
for my life; it is so much higher than my own. Restore
hope and bring new vision to my life. Show me where to
walk and what to do. Oh, Jesus, let me know the Father's
heart for His people.*

*Help me step out in faith with a boldness worthy
of the Lion of Judah. Fill my mouth with Your words.
Thank you, for helping me press on to contend for
the miracles I need in my life, and to grow, so I can
encourage others in their quest. Stir in my heart a deep
desire to constantly be about Your business. Give me a
heart for the people You send me; for those in my sphere
of influence, and for those for whom I need to step out
of my comfort zone and into the world. I am ready,
Lord, send me. I pray this in Jesus' name. Amen.*

# CHAPTER FOUR

# Panama City

PULLING ON THE DOOR HANDLE, I ENTERED THE GREEN Spot, a quaint corner coffee shop located at the base of a large apartment tower. It was my intent to arrive early enough to familiarize myself with the new environment before the rest of my party was scheduled to arrive. Being visually impaired, this helps me prepare for the upcoming interaction and avoid potentially embarrassing mishaps. This time though, as I entered the coffee shop, Rod and Roy were already waiting.

Rod warmly greeted me and introduced me to Roy. We shook hands, ordered a coffee, and sat at a small round table. We each shared a little bit about ourselves and talked about the organization, *Leader Impact*, with which Roy and Rod were involved. Then Roy slid a piece of paper across the table. Though a seemingly casual act, this paper had huge implications that would impact my entire being and lead me to the next step in God's plan for my life.

Though I am unable to read text, I soon discovered the paper was an invitation to join with Leader Impact in a global exchange to be held in Panama City, in the nation of Panama. As Roy began to explain the dynamics of the exchange, something leapt inside of me in anticipation. I turned to Rod and said, "Do you know who I think should come to this?" and he responded with one name—Dale. Dale is my father-in-law, and his thought echoed my own. We concluded coffee, and I agreed to pray about it and promised to talk with Dale.

Arriving home, I excitedly discussed it with my wife, then called my father-in-law to extend the invitation. The response I received on the other end of the phone was not exactly what I had anticipated; more like dull shock than excited enthusiasm. I suggested he think about it, and then I disconnected. What followed was several months of persistent nudging and encouraging from me, met by stubborn resistance from Dale. I recognized a serious spiritual battle happening in his life; God was encouraging Dale to step out into what He had created him to do, and Dale was battling with all of the lies and insecurities trying to prevent him from doing this very thing. After several weeks, Dale finally agreed to come to Panama, alongside his wife, Patti. I was ecstatic about Dale's choice; not only could they help me navigate the new environment, but I believed God was opening a new door in their lives.

Finally, the day came to board the plane to Panama City. As per usual for me, my mind raced with potential disasters that could occur on an excursion to a new destination—scenarios like a gigantic spider crawling on me while I'm sleeping, or a gang of thugs taking over the hotel. These absurd scenarios, however, never prove to be true.

Panama, as it turned out, was a modern city and we stayed in a pleasant hotel.

The focus of a global exchange is to bring in business leaders from different countries to share strategies linked with something called a *faith story*. A faith story is your testimony encapsulated in three minutes or less. It's a tremendous tool for equipping people to share the things God has done in their lives, with the purpose of leading people to Jesus. I met some of the other business people as they arrived at the hotel one by one, which helped me begin to recognize them by name and voice.

During a time of prayer the first morning, I truly grasped the broad spectrum of people participating in this exchange. There were eighteen of us from all over the world, coming from different socioeconomic backgrounds. We were all believers, but represented different denominations. I was the youngest man in the group, but the age range was widespread. The stark contrast between the individuals in the group amplified the awesomeness of what was about to take place over the next several days.

The global exchange began with three days of intense training as we learned how to develop our faith stories and to deliver business talks. The entire group was shut into a single room from morning until night in training, much like a sequestered jury during a controversial trial. From the very first day, the Holy Spirit's presence was apparent in the room. As the introduction to the exchange occurred, in my mind I started to plan out the parameters of my faith story. The one thing I did not share with people, COULD NOT share with people was that I was visually impaired.

I could talk about the dysfunction in my home growing up, the physical abuse I suffered, and the drugs I used to anesthetize my pain. I could share how poor I had been and tell of how my family often ate from the trashcan to survive. The one thing I could not share was that I was legally blind. Sharing about my impairment would be too much; it would leave me too vulnerable. I have spent most of my life avoiding the truth that I was in the process of losing my eyesight. I strived to build a successful business and prove to everyone I was good enough to be loved and I was capable of providing for the needs of those close to me. In this way, I attempted to make up for the deep deficit I felt in my heart caused by being legally blind.

A few months before going to Panama, I felt God asking me to share my testimony and to be open to speaking when opportunity arose. For this reason I came to Panama: to share my testimony with the local people. I would encourage them that they too, can face mountainous struggles in their lives and emerge victoriously, as I had. The one thing I did not plan to address was my eyesight. I did not consider this something which I have triumphed over, but rather a weakness, a failure I needed to hide. After all, as a believer, I thought, *Should God not have healed me by now? What did I do wrong?* Somehow, I believed it was my fault, so I hid it away in shame, and I was not open to sharing my failure with anyone. I was willing to speak from my mind, but unwilling to share from my heart.

On the second day of this intense process, my heart began shifting. Roy, our table leader, encouraged me to be forthcoming about my impairment. He thought I was inspiring, accomplishing what I had accomplished, despite the challenges. So, after some coaxing—maybe even cajoling—I made the monumental decision to include it in my faith story.

As the day progressed and the stories were developed, one by one, people began to share. My heart was deeply moved by what I heard—from terrible childhoods, to painful losses, to years of believing lies the devil whispered to them, inflicting pain upon their hearts. One after the other, men and women who I consider to be business giants, stood up and poured out their hearts. The tears spilled over as the intimate details of people's lives were put on the altar for all to see. The metaphorical gauge in my heart—my bravery gauge, my ability to share the truth—surged from empty to full.

With the complete exposure of my heart imminent, my turn was upon me. I stood up, and for the first time in my life, opened up about my testimony … *all* of my testimony. I talked about everything from my childhood, to my adolescence, to the loss of our dear niece, Kailey Grace, to meningitis. Then I cautiously spoke about losing my sight. I found myself confessing the anger I felt toward God because of it, catching myself by surprise. Though I could not yet say out loud that I was blind, I identified my lack of understanding as to why He did not heal me. *Did God the Father not truly love me?* The depth of my pain became apparent as the tears streamed down my face. This was the onset of my miracle—the identification of my trust wound. I did not trust God to be a good Father.

There was a special grace in that room as lives were shared and unity was built. One by one, I saw people's hearts and lives begin a miraculous transformation. I've learned that these moments are extremely precious when they happen. It's a divine intersection where God meets with His people, and He releases His grace and mercy to flow. I watched as broken people entered one way and left another, transformed by the power of God.

One personal friend of mine, Kevin, came in broken and hurting because of a painful situation in his life. It was incredible to watch the process unfold as God took this man from the painful situation he was in, and eventually honored him in the unlikeliest of places—the presidential palace of Panama. Wow! Dale and Patti had also chosen to step out, sharing their stories and being activated to pursue their own God adventure. Over the week, I saw them reach an incredible new threshold; one which has left them forever changed.

The week resumed with various dinners and speaking engagements, but I know in my heart I was predominantly there to become part of a family, to encourage and empower the team of believers to engage with what God was calling them to do. Throughout the week, many heart connections were made, and my spiritual family grew with new moms and dads, aunts and uncles, and sisters and brothers being added. It was one of those rare, phenomenal experiences when you wish you could just pause time and remain in the grace and companionship within the group.

Inevitably, the last day arrived, and it came time to place our Ebenezer memorial stones. Earlier in the week, the group leaders had asked us to pick up a stone to be used as a memento of our time in Panama. The events we witnessed, the places we went, and the lives we helped change were incredible; there was much to be celebrated and remembered with our stones. God used this special group to shape and change the very nation of Panama (Joshua 4).

On this last day, the time had come to place my Ebenezer stone with the others at the front of the room, and share my moment of greatest impact during the week. I ensured I went last. I needed to tell this group how much love they had poured out for me and how it had brought about a transformation that would never be undone. I walked to the front with my stone that had been picked up, fittingly, by Roy. He had retrieved it from in front of St. Michael's Hospital, in a city in which I had spoken a couple of times. The stone was profoundly significant to me; it represented a miracle of healing in my heart.

I stood there, tapping the stone on the table as a flush crept up my cheeks and tears rolled from my eyes. For the first-time ever, I was able to share out loud, that I was blind and that I accepted the fact that it was not God who did this to me. I acknowledged that God was not angry with me, and He was, instead, causing things in my life to work together for my good. Although it might seem like a simple premise for most believers, when struggling with a disability, it is a revelation and a breakthrough. One small stone and one short week in the city of Panama forever altered the direction of my life.

Now, I see myself as an accepted son of God, and I am able to embrace the calling He has for my life. I began the journey of learning to trust Him with my *whole* heart. Trip concluded, plane boarded, I was on my way home ... home with my miracle. Yet Panama was merely the on-ramp to an amazing sequence of events, lined up like dominos, by our creative Designer.

## Insight:

We all have giants in our lives which appear much like Goliath; that giant who confidently strutted into the valley and taunted the nation of Israel. He dismissed their significance, telling them how weak and incapable they were—undeniably inept at facing him in battle. They were unable to trust the Lord to give them the victory.

Instilling in us a lack of trust is still a favorite tactic of the enemy. He tries to push us into a corner of fear so we will not fight back, possibly not even show up for the fight. The truth is, God has already given us everything we need to defeat the giants in our lives. Like David using a slingshot and a simple stone to defeat Goliath, we have the rock, who is Jesus Christ. He has paid the price to give us victory over every giant that tries to stand in our way. We need to trust Him, rise up and walk out that victory to silence the taunting giants. Your giant may be insecurity, a disability, past failures, or a myriad of other hindrances. Giants come in all shapes and sizes, but they all have been defeated by Jesus. Arise, put your trust in the Lord, and defeat your giants right now!

## PRAYER:

*Heavenly Father, I come before You with my heart in my hands, ready to place it on the altar. I am ready for my transformational moment. I am ready to engage with the destiny You have designed especially for me. I ask You to help me prepare my faith story, so I will always be ready to give account for what I believe, and so I can share what You have done in and through my life.*

*I ask You to give me the courage to be vulnerable and able to express my heart to You and to others, so You can bring all the healing I need, and extend it to those around me. Teach me to trust You, Lord, even when I don't understand. As I open my heart to You, I thank You for bringing about the miraculous healing and transformation I need so I can do all You have planned for me to do. Thank you for Your grace and mercy that flow as I begin to walk in this.*

*Make me brave! I ask for revelation that will expose all the wounds I carry and all the lies I believe. Show me the root of these lies that have created strongholds in my life, keeping me in bondage. I repent for partnering with these lies, and I turn away from walking in them. Lord,*

*I ask that You dismantle any walls and structures I have built as I have partnered with these lies, keeping You and others out of those areas of my heart. Replace the faulty foundation of my life with the firm foundation of Your truth.*

*Thank you for the breakthroughs I need to overcome my struggles, and the barriers and the hindrances I face—my giants, as I walk the road on which You have put me. Thank you for already giving me everything I need to be the conqueror You have called me to be.*

*I thank You for bringing people into my life to help me in my journey. I ask that You continue putting those on my path that I can encourage, and the ones that will encourage me. Help me, Lord, to fully receive Your love, and see myself as an accepted son/daughter of God. Help me to embrace the calling You have on my life, and trust You with my whole heart, knowing that we already have the victory. Help me rise up, for with You, I am strong in battle. I pray this in the mighty name of the Lord Jesus Christ. Amen*

# CHAPTER FIVE

# "GO!"

THE PROPHETIC IS OFTEN USED AS A CATALYST FOR the moving of the Holy Spirit. We see a biblical example of this prophetic voice in John 4 as Jesus rests at Jacob's well in a Samaritan village. While he conversed with a local woman who had come to draw water, He began to tell her intimate details about her life. Amazed, she ran back into town, proclaiming to everyone that they should meet this incredible prophet who had told her everything she has done. Curiosity provoked, the villagers sought out Jesus for themselves, wanting to hear more of what He had to say. They begged Him to stay with them for a few days—revival was the profound result.

This encounter provides a concrete example of the critical nature of knowing how to hear God's voice. When we know how to listen carefully, we can confidently act on behalf of His will. We must believe God *will* speak to His people, and He honestly desires to do so. Like a continuously broadcasting radio station, God is *always* speaking to us—all of us, not just the prophets. Our role is to tune into the right frequency and listen to what He is saying. In this way, we open the door to miracles. The Bible promises us that if we seek, we shall find, and if we knock, the door will be opened unto us (Matthew 7:7). This next story is the outcome of tuning into the right frequency and hearing the voice of God.

Sitting in my office one day, I received a *WhatsApp* call from my good friend Marco, from Germany. He wanted prayer for direction about whether or not he should go to Guatemala to speak at a conference. I typically do not pray to this end, but Marco is a very good friend, so I agreed. I disconnected and went to pray. In my mind, I quickly saw a big green *GO* and then the name *Hernandez*. Then I saw a road going from the big city, through the jungle, and on to a small town. I felt God was going to take him from the city to a small town as part of his journey. These images were accompanied by a sense of promise for God's provision.

I phoned Marco and told him all the Lord had shown me. He laughed and shared that he had been invited to minister in a small jungle church in Panama while en route. Marco thanked me and determined he was going to step out in faith. A few days later, he called me again, chuckling. He wanted to share a shocking revelation. On the conference website, spelled out in big, green letters, was its name—the "GO" Conference.

The day had come to travel to Guatemala, and Marco, led by faith, embarked on this trip halfway across the world to speak at the conference. And God, ever true to His Word, marked the trip with His provision. At the conference, Marco shared the word he had received from me with the pastors, and how those words had encouraged him to step out in faith. The one female pastor laughingly said, "Marco, don't you know, my last name is Hernandez!" This was yet another strong affirmation of what God was doing, and going to do in Panama!

However, the biggest miracle took place in the small jungle church. While Marco was there, several people from the hosting church took him for lunch at a local restaurant. The Lord interrupted their conversation with a word of knowledge. He told Marco that the waitress had pain in her feet. She confirmed the pain when he asked, and allowed him to pray for her. Her feet were instantly healed! In shock, the waitress asked how he was able to do this. Marco simply replied, "It is God. He loves you."

The manager of the restaurant, however, did not like the event that had transpired. She made several derogatory, sarcastic comments toward Marco. The next time the manager approached, Marco bluntly faced her and declared, "Your father is sick, and God is going to heal him. I need to talk to your father right now." Taken aback, she replied, "You don't understand. My father has not spoken a word in years." Marco gently insisted she phone him immediately, because he needed to speak with him. Reluctantly, the manager agreed and called her father. Marco had a beautiful conversation with this man—this man who had Alzheimer's, a lost memory, and had not spoken in years. The manager was completely undone by this miracle. With tears in her eyes, she shut down the entire restaurant for the rest of the day, designating it a holy place, and together they praised God. Astounding! How great is our God!

When the manager arrived home that night, she heard for herself that her father was speaking in his right mind and had indeed, been healed! The entire family was astonished, and they all wanted to receive Christ! Taking up Marco's invitation from the night before to come to the church service, the manager and seventeen of her family members showed up the next morning. Though the building was packed, the church members very graciously cleared out the front row so the family could sit and listen to Marco speak. Not only was this a miraculous work of God healing the physical, but also healing spiritually through salvations.

## INSIGHT:

The most fascinating aspects of this particular miracle were its connection between several people on different continents, and that it originated through a prophetic word from God. The Lord often uses prophecy to confirm a word He has already placed in people's hearts. Even more amazing is that the Bible says all can prophesy. God promises "it shall come to pass ..., that I will pour out my Spirit on all flesh; your sons and your daughters shall prophesy" (Joel 2:28 ESV). Obedience to these prophetic words is key. God will speak to us, and when He does, we must listen and follow through by immediately doing what He requests. John 9:4 states that we must "quickly carry out the tasks assigned to us" (NLT). We need to believe in our hearts that He will not fail, and do what He asks.

Along with speaking directly to us, the Holy Spirit may

also speak to us through the prophetic words of someone else. If this is the case, it is important not to naïvely accept that everything you are told *is* from the Lord; do confirm it. Remember, God will always confirm His Word. He will often confirm it through another person, but He will *always* confirm it with Scripture. Once you believe the word you received is from the Lord, it is important to step out in faith and in obedience. This is the exact faith-step Marco took by going to Panama, and as a result, we both became an integral part of more than one incredible miracle!

We need to have ears to hear and eyes to see when the Lord is calling us to act or speak. If you have never given or even received a prophetic word, I strongly encourage you to explore this area. I suggest receiving some training through a healthy church that shepherds the prophetic as well. One such resource is *www.dianeharrison.com*. Diane leads the prophetic ministry in my home church, Harvest City Church, in Regina, Saskatchewan, Canada, and she travels the world to bring this training to the nations. Let's pray.

## PRAYER:

*Lord, it is such an exciting journey as we become imitators of Jesus! Thank you for Your provision as we walk this journey of faith together. Lord, I ask You to open my eyes and ears so I can hear Your voice ever more clearly. Take off any veils or blinders deposited by the enemy. Help me, Lord, to keep my heart open to*

*Your Word. Bind up any spirits that come against me, attempting to harden my heart. Reveal any sin in my life that will push me off the way You have for me.*

*I ask You to grow my knowledge, understanding, and practise of the prophetic, so I can be instrumental in Your plans for the people You have ordained to be in my life. Help me to be a faithful steward of this gift. Activate new prophetic gifts in my life so I can be more effective in Your kingdom, and draw all men unto You. Lord, I ask You to bring the resources I need: people, books, videos, events, or anything else You provide, so I can be fully trained in hearing Your voice and walking in the prophetic.*

*Lord God, I receive Your Spirit as You pour it out on me. Spark in me a determination to always be obedient and quickly follow through with all You have designated me to do. I bind up any obstacles that attempt to deter me. Increase my faith daily, Lord. Thank you for all You have done for me, and for all the trust You have placed in me. In Jesus' name, I walk in confidence. Amen.*

# CHAPTER SIX

# The Boardroom

To this point, the described miracles have changed individual lives and shaped the destiny of families for generations to come. Within these miracles lies the evidence that God cares about the individual and the family. But God is a big God, and His plans also entail shaping the destiny of nations. The Old Testament demonstrates how masterfully God weaves the destinies of individuals, families, and nations together through the power of the Holy Spirit in the working of miracles.

The life of God's servant, Moses, was transformed by such power, through the miracle of the burning bush. This incredible interaction altered the course of Moses' life. It set off a chain reaction that led Moses to recruit his brother, Aaron, and bring their entire family to the palace of Egypt. Here, they petitioned Pharaoh to release the nation of Israel so its people could be free to worship the Lord. The Israelites were released from captivity, and Moses was the one who led the Exodus.

In the New Testament, God continued this tapestry by sending His only begotten Son, so that whoever would believe in Him would receive eternal life (John 3:16). Jesus paid the ultimate price so the mercy of God can be shown to individuals, families, and nations, so that they might be able to accept Him as their Lord and Savior. God has great interest in seeing everyone come to Him to receive His mercy and His blessing.

The next miracle in the sequence of my life unfolded while I was ministering in one such nation that desperately needed the Lord's mercy and guidance. I was part of a team tasked with giving business talks in this nation's capital city of several million people. We had been invited to several venues to deliver these talks, in conjunction with our faith stories. One of these venues was City Hall, and we were designated to speak to some municipal leaders that govern the large city. Dale and Patti, my father and mother-in-law, along with Brad and Dwayne—my good friends and brothers in the Lord—were all a part of the team joining me at this event. This country, although democratic, has a very strong president who has ruled the nation for many years. Our host for the day was the executive director, who was the head of the group, and reported directly to this president.

Upon arriving at City Hall, our vehicle pulled up to a large metal gate, obviously designed to prevent malicious people from infiltrating the property. Security was paramount due to the veritable threat of vehicles carrying bombs, requiring us to exit our van. Leaving the vehicle at the gate, we walked through a metal detector before proceeding to the next checkpoint. After ascending the marble steps leading to the entrance of City Hall, we once again had to avail ourselves to yet another metal detector. Security in this building was in no way lax.

The guards were friendly, showing big smiles as they welcomed us to their city's center of power. This made bearable the very intrusive process of being searched and subjecting ourselves to the detectors. Once inside, we walked through a foyer that opened into a large, bright atrium filled with tropical plants. On the right was a door leading to the room where our meeting was to be held. The room was packed, containing a large boardroom table around which sat the executive director and the municipal leaders—representing each district of the city—along with their entourages.

Our program design for the day was straightforward: Brad was to speak, I would follow him, we would end with a short prayer, and be on our way. But that was not all the Holy Spirit had in mind. His plan was that much greater—inconceivable from a human perspective. Brad was fantastic, delivering an eloquent and powerful speech about the necessity of speaking truth to power. He ended his allotted time with his personal faith story, capable of moving the hardest of individuals. Then it was my turn. I arose and began to share my message of leadership. I had originally planned, as always, to conclude with my personal faith story.

As I neared the end of my faith story, I heard the Holy Spirit tell me not to pray for salvation, but instead, to pray for people to receive the Father's love. In obedience, I asked everyone in the room to bow their heads and close their eyes. I explained that if what I had said had resonated within them and they wished to receive the Father's love, then, being brave, raise their hands, and I would pray for them. Almost all of the municipal leaders and many in their entourages raised their hands. I could sense God was moving in the room as I prayed. My heart was full and my eyes were anything but dry.

We concluded our meeting and shook many hands. The executive director then invited the team to come to his office, located a few levels higher in the building. We went through two more checkpoints with metal detectors and continued until we reached a corner office at the end of a long hallway. The office was modern; indistinguishable from that of a mayor's office in any North American city. It was spacious, containing a large desk and a small boardroom table. Once in the room, the director invited us to sit at the table, where he offered us some drinks. He sat down and began to share an epic story—one of the most incredible accounts of struggle and divine intervention I had ever heard in my life. The intriguing chronicle that unfolded outlined the director's life journey. Everything he had undergone highlighted the undeniable providence of God's involvement that had led him to this exact point and position in his life. It was simply amazing, but because of confidentiality, I cannot share the details.

What I can share, is that God used our talks to speak to a situation he and the president were facing; challenges that would affect the entire nation. He had been seeking guidance from the Lord about the appropriate action to take.

When the director wound down his tale, the presence of God in the room was tangible. I asked if I could pray into the situation and see what the Lord would say. The director agreed, and I began to pray. God provided both Dwayne and me with prophetic words that spoke specifically into the situation the director currently faced. The words gave him encouragement and direction regarding what was happening in the nation. The Lord also spoke through the other team members, with words of wisdom and encouragement. We spoke truth, hope, and love into the situation. The Lord was speaking to this powerful individual about the next steps that would unfold. We ended up ministering for two and a half hours. The tears bore witness to the powerful move of God that had befallen.

It was incredible that God chose to touch an entire nation through our team's interaction with this individual at that point in time. Since some time has passed from when the event transpired, I can confirm that the words spoken by the Lord have begun to come to pass, and God is moving in that nation. I believe God is far from finished, and there's much more to be done. The Lord not only reaffirmed to this individual His love for him, but also provided comfort at an extremely difficult time.

## INSIGHT:

God has a heart for individuals, for families, and for nations. Matthew 10:18 makes it evident that we will be brought before the leaders of the nations, with the opportunity to share about Christ. This is a terrifying thought for many people. Studies have shown that the number one fear, even surpassing that of death, is the fear of public speaking. As Christians, we can take great comfort that the Holy Spirit will be the One who fills our mouth so we do not have to worry about what we will say (Matthew 10:18–19). Therefore, though we should prepare for these opportunities, we need not be fearful or anxious beforehand, nor during the moment, but trust that the Lord will give us the words we need to speak.

Although the team and I were not under arrest when we came before this leader, as often was the case in the Scriptures, the Holy Spirit gave us words to help change the destiny of that nation. God can bring such intervention in many ways. The event in which Joseph interpreted the dream for Pharaoh gives evidence of this. We need to be courageous and willing to speak truth to power. We cannot allow fear and intimidation to hold us back from the steps of faith God is calling us to take.

Another facet of this miracle which I loved, was that Dale and Patti were with me to witness this incredible event. It blessed me in a way that is almost inexpressible. They too, did not just sit and watch; they were brave and stepped out, allowing the Holy Spirit to speak words of wisdom and encouragement through them. This is yet another testament of God's amazing plan for our lives.

As you've progressed through this book, you've seen examples of God performing a miracle for an individual. Then you've read of how He performed a miracle in a family, and now, how He's using the individual and the family to transform nations! Sound familiar? How great is our God! He has a plan for you and for your family too! The fact that God would use individuals like my colleagues, my family and me, to help shape the destiny of a nation—placing the miracle in our hands—is a miracle in itself. I am honored and humbled. We are nothing special; we simply said, "Yes," chose to be courageous, and were available. Are you?

## PRAYER:

*Lord God, Creator of the Heavens, thank you for the depth of Your love. Thank you for showing such mercy to Your servants that You have already paid the price of our sin through Your Son, Jesus Christ. Thank you that we are now free to receive the fullness of Your love. Help me to receive it, Lord, to the depths of my soul, so I can be fully healed and set free, and can lead others to this same place of victory. Thank you for desiring for each one of us to walk in the fullness of our destiny, right down through our generational line. Thank you for the power of the Holy Spirit, through whom You weave together destinies that will transform the life not only of individuals, but also that of families and entire nations.*

*Thank you, Lord, for leading us and guiding us in every way, and for the plans You have for us, that are so much greater than what we can conceive on our own. Thank you for speaking into the challenges we face daily, whether the implications of the situation are on an individual, or a national scale. Thank you for giving us words of wisdom so we can encourage one another, and bear one another's burdens, speaking hope, truth, comfort, and love into one another's lives.*

*I am truly humbled and honored that You would choose to partner with me, putting me before everyone from everyday people like myself, to kings and queens, so I can share Christ with them, love them, and encourage them, impacting nations as I do. I pray You unlock my mouth, so words will flow from the Holy Spirit—words that are transformational for entire countries.*

*I thank You that even now You are stirring my heart, causing me to have a passion for the people group for whom You have chosen me to be a mouth-piece. Make me fearless. I command anxiety and intimidation to "Go," in Jesus' name! I command fear to leave, in Jesus' name. Make me bold and brave so I can stand up and engage with what You are calling me to do. I ask You to overcome me with a Spirit of boldness, so I can be part of changing the very fabric of nations.*

*Your Word says You have not given us a spirit of fear, but of peace and a sound mind. I pray You release this Spirit of peace and a sound mind over me and all those around me. I ask this all in the mighty name of Jesus. Amen.*

# CHAPTER SEVEN

# God of Miracles

As I stepped onto the red African dirt in Uganda, approximately four hours south of the equator, my mind filled with disappointment. The Muslim governor of the district had called a last-minute holiday that wiped out the entire day of business meetings we had set up for our team from North America. Along with the crusades during the evenings, our team of Christian business leaders was to share practical business advice, faith stories, and Jesus with the leaders of the district. The last-minute Muslim holiday scuttled all of this.

As a consolation, the owner of our hotel suggested we explore the hot springs, located fifteen minutes away. He laughingly suggested perhaps we could preach there. The translator from the previous night's crusade was meeting with my pastor, and decided to accompany us. Oddly enough, as we walked to the van he said, "When you preach, I will translate for you." I laughed, replying that I was not preaching today. Besides, my pastor was the evangelist on this trip, not I.

As I now walked on the red African soil at the hot springs, I looked around. With my peripheral vision, I could see large rocks surrounding two pools of water. One pool was larger than the other. Navigating the large rocks, inclines, and declines was very difficult with my visual impairment. A couple of team members led me around to the small spring of water. The water came from an underground stream that was heated by a local volcano and was very hot to the touch. While this was happening, the Holy Spirit spoke to me about preaching the gospel in this place.

Imagine the scene with me. It was right out of a National Geographic film. The hot springs were surrounded by rocks all the way around and filled with African tribal people who came from every direction, some from many miles away. The local belief is that the waters have healing powers and if you were to bathe in them, you could be healed. These people were poor and desperate. I knew the water had no healing power, but Jesus could heal them. He was their only hope. I was stirred with compassion. Half-jokingly, I asked the interpreter if we could preach here. He hurried off and talked to whom I assumed was the chief of the area, and obtained permission for us to do so.

That was it. In an instant, I was committed. I had a choice either to do it scared, or to look like a fool. It had been my dream for many years to preach the gospel, and now the opportunity was directly presented to me. A choice lay before me. What was I going to do?

Choice made, I climbed up on a large rock, facing the people in the bigger pool. As I took those few steps, the only explanation for what happened next, was that the Holy Spirit rose up within me. I was not nervous, but rather, felt empowered. My interpreter mounted a rock to my left, and one of my team members crouched down in front to prevent me from falling into the water.

I began to preach, declaring a simple, but powerful message about Jesus and His healing powers. I recounted the story about the pool of Bethesda (John 5) in which the first person to descend into the water after the angel stirred it, would be healed. I explained that Jesus died for our sins, and if they invited Him from the outside to the inside, He would forgive all their sins and heal all their diseases—every one of them. I preached for only about five minutes and then made a call for salvation. One hundred percent of an estimated two hundred souls gave their lives to Jesus! I did not stop there, but was compelled to pray for healing, since my message assured them He could heal all of their diseases. At first I was calling them out of the water, not realizing many of them were naked! One of my team members quickly suggested a general prayer. I prayed, and many people said they were healed right then and there.

After the general prayer, countless people left the water, dressed, and came up to us for more specific healing needs. The miracles began, and many diseases were healed. I personally witnessed two blind ladies receive their sight, just like that. This had an incredible impact on me due to my own visual impairment. I don't profess to understand how healing works; I just know God still heals today. We saw a woman limp up to us, dragging her crippled leg behind her. This leg lacked most of its muscle mass. Right under our praying hands, we could feel the muscles grow back, and she walked away under the power of both legs. Dozens of other miracles were performed as our entire team prayed in unity over the people. It was like a scene from the Book of Acts. One of our team members gave a Bible to a man who professed he would plant a church on that very spot. If I had not been there and it wasn't captured on video, I would have had a hard time believing it myself. But God is an amazing God, and He longs to do amazing things through all of us.

When we left the hot springs, we were pursued by a man yelling and demanding money. Our interpreter informed us he was the local witch doctor, and we had just put him out of business. Driving back to our hotel with my mind racing, all that would come out of my mouth was, "Wow!" I had connected with something huge. I had connected with my destiny. It didn't look like I had imagined, but I knew in my heart, it was where I had to be.

## INSIGHT:

I had taken a big risk, and I had done it afraid. I had boldly stepped out in obedience, and completed the task the Lord set before me at that moment in time. We can be released from fear, but we must learn to consciously step out in boldness. We need to climb upon the rock of ages, Jesus, and proclaim that He is who He says He is—the rock of our salvation and we will not be moved! Matthew 11:12 clearly states that the Kingdom suffers violence and the violent take it by force. This is how chains are broken and captives are set free! It is time for you to arise and engage with the call God has destined for your life. Unleash His miracle-working power, and step out!

## PRAYER:

*Dear Lord, let the excitement grow in my belly as I learn to walk closer and closer with You. Thank you for all You have been teaching me. Thank you for increasing my faith. I ask You to open up the vision for my life. Birth in me the dreams You have planted in my heart long ago, and engage me in the destiny to which You have called me.*

*Thank you that as my walk with You grows tighter, I can commit to doing Your will, even if I'm scared. Thank you that I can trust Your guidance. Help me to see every opportunity You place before me, and grant me the courage to jump in, without hesitation, trusting You to catch me. Train me up and make me so bold, that taking the big risks are no different than taking the little ones.*

*Father, baptize me with Your Holy Spirit power. Send Your fire upon me. Free me from all fear! Raise me up to be that warrior who can take ground for Your Kingdom by force! Let me be one of the warriors You call upon to break chains and set captives free! Lord, God, unleash Your miracle-working power in me so I can war with You to bring Heaven to earth. I humbly pray this in the name above all names, Jesus Christ.*

## COMMISSIONING PRAYER:

Father, I thank You that You are the God of miracles! Lord, I come before You in the name of Jesus and I ask You to touch this reader right now, filling them with the baptism of the Holy Spirit. Father, I pray You would fill them from the top of their head to the soles of their feet, and the tips of their fingers. I pray You renew and refresh Your Spirit in them, and allow Your miracle-working power to flow through them. I thank You, God, that even right now we would come into agreement and believe for the gift of miracles to be activated in this reader.

Father, I thank You that this reader would rise up in great boldness, lay hold of Your promises, and see themselves as more than a conqueror. Reveal to them their true identity in Christ, and the position of authority this identity grants to them. Let them see that they are the head, and not the tail. I thank You that they would take authority through You over demonic forces, strongholds, powers and principalities, so chains may be broken and captives set free. Bestow upon them the power to enforce the dominion of Christ throughout the earth. Help them to see Thy Kingdom come, in Jesus' name! Expand Your Kingdom upon the earth through Your people, Lord!

I come into agreement with the reader for each miracle they are contending for in their life. I say, "Yes and amen." I also come into agreement with them in believing for the miracles they need in the lives of their family members. I thank You for the amazing, life-changing testimonies of miracles. Father, I thank You that even now You are placing people they don't even know into their paths so they would have the opportunity to step out in obedience and believe You for miracles.

Father, I thank You for ordaining each reader to come across my own path so we may become part of each other's stories. I believe You want to use them in mighty, powerful ways. God, I thank You for giving the reader the courage to step out, to lay hands on people, and believe for miracles. I bless them. Shower Your mercy and grace upon them. I pray this in the mighty name of Jesus Christ. AMEN!

If this book has blessed you, would you help me out by leaving a review by clicking the link below. Even a one sentence review will help the book get into the hands of other readers and bless them too. Thank you in advance!

*www.amazon.com/God-Miracles*
*-Ordinary-Extraordinary-Stories-ebook/*
*product-reviews/B0786WG4QQ*

**Jeff Barnhardt** is a husband to Andrea and a father of four children. He is a best selling author, speaker, and award-winning entrepreneur. He has ministered to the body of Christ and business leaders in many countries around the world. Jeff currently serves as president and CEO of a privately held security company he founded with his wife.

His passion is to help people discover their life's purpose while empowering them to unlock their God-given potential.

Connect with Jeff at:

Website: *www.jeffbarnhardt.com*
Facebook: *www.facebook.com/JeffRBarnhardt*
Twitter: *@jeff_barnhardt*

# DESTINED *to* BE

**NINE KEYS *to* LIVE A LIFE OF PURPOSE**
*While* **UNLOCKING YOUR FULL POTENTIAL**

# JEFF BARNHARDT